a deeply personal story of embracing flaws.

Stardust and Skin

by Carla M. Cherry

iiPUBLISHING

Stardust and Skin
Copyright © 2020 by Carla M. Cherry

Copyright notice
All rights reserved. No part of this book may be reproduced in any form or by any electronic or mechanical means, including information storage and retrieval systems, without permission in writing from the author or publisher, except for the use of brief quotations in a book review.

Cover & Illustrations copyright © 2020 by tonii

ISBN: 978-0-578-78675-9

Printed in the United States of America

iiPUBLISHING

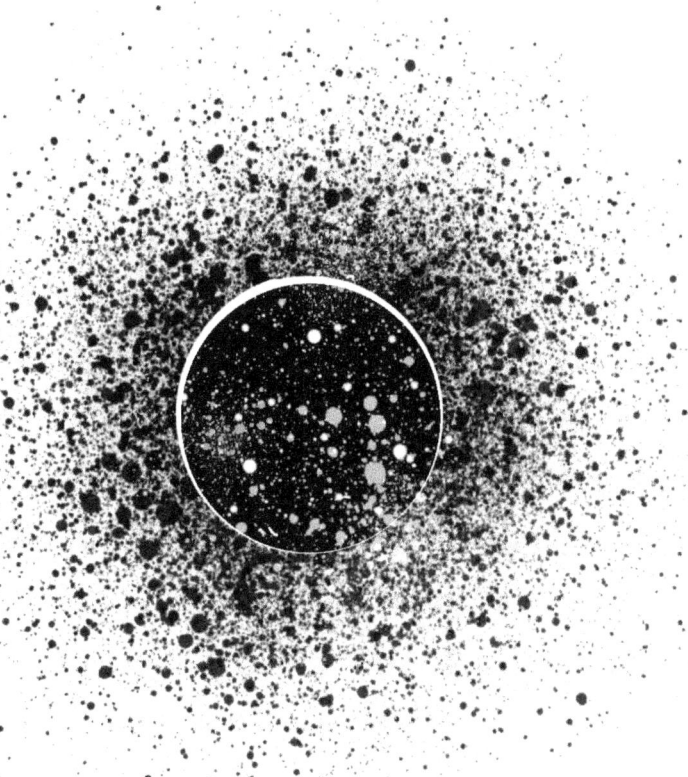

Stardust and Skin was inspired by poet Peggy Robles-Alvarado and her Robleswrites Productions multi-media workshop, "More Than Just". Its purpose was to bring women of color together to engage in healing exercises, celebrate themselves beyond being daughters, sisters, mothers, or wives, participate in a photo shoot, and share their experiences with their communities-at-large.

"More Than Just" was a beautiful, inspirational experience. Thank you Vanessa Chica! A very special thanks to Lillibeth Gonzalez for your meticulous and fulfilling make-up session during the photo shoot. Peggy, thank you for the gorgeous photographs, and Tamara G. Saliva, thank you for your photo editing skills.

I also want to thank my best friend, Dr. Tanya Manning-Yarde, and my mentor, Rainmaker, for your guidance and multiple readings of my poems. I love you both so much!

I dedicate this book to my mother, my son Khari, my niece Anike, the memory of my father, and to my beloved sister Donna who joined the Village of the Ancestors on November 20, 2018. I love you and miss you always.

Ashe

Table of Contents

Grand	2
To Make It So	4
Waylaid	6
Pluck	8
When We Answered the Call	10
Sap	12
Cracked	14
Ingress	18
Veneer	21
My Honey Jar	22
Lost	24
Light	27
Weight	28
The Spiritual Bath	30
On My Knees	32
Grace	37
Sermon	40
Wonder	43
War on Canvas	44
Manna	50
Pass It On	52
Next	54
Afterword	59
About the Author	61

Black girls, don't forget the joy
that wraps around you in your skin.

Grand

Seated by the entrance to our Sister Circle,
a wide white wrap around her head,
her dark brown locs flowing outward,
wearing a white cotton A-line dress,
white shoes,
our facilitator instructs:

"Take this white paper.
Write down something you need to heal
in your wombs and fold it."

We write in silence.
I record the names of my regrets.

"You will walk over to the small table
in the center of our circle,
place that wound
into the glass container filled with water,
and as each of you does so, say,
Ashe."

"What has brought all of you here?"
One by one, we declare:

A need for inner peace.
Healing from a breakup.
Dispose of negative energy.
Forgiveness.
Resurrection of creativity.

"I wasn't going to come except for this sister,"
a woman says, gesturing to her right.
"My daughter died a few months ago.
My other daughter is in the hospital.

I am angry. I am sad. I have trouble getting out of bed,
and I feel bad because my sick daughter needs me.
I don't know what to do."

You are so strong, I say.
I just lost my sister before last Thanksgiving.
My mother has the same anger and sadness that you
       do.
You're doing the best you can.
Don't be afraid to ask for help.
Heads nod, tissues pass, cheeks are wiped
because we know
our shawl of sympathetic words and tears
may not do much to keep her warm
and will not rush grief along.

"Before you go," the leader says,
"reach inside your white gift bags."

We each pull out the stone
from its tiny white canvas bag.

The stone was white.
"It's a moonstone," she says.
"Choose a goal".

I want to keep writing.

We embrace each other,
exchange names once more,
drink fresh squeezed apple juice with wheatgrass,
and one by one,
prance Harlem pavement
with halcyon feet.

To Make It So

I put the moonstone
in the center of my right hand, squeezed like
it was my morning grapefruit,
with every wedge of pulp pulled
from pith and membrane,
every drop of juice falling into my bowl.

Waylaid

He jumped into my path with a tube of sea scrub in his
       hand.
"Come look."

I'm sorry, but I'm on a budget.

He gently took my hand.
He was young, handsome, brown as a coconut husk.

Smoothed the scrub onto my forearm.
It tickled in a way that made me wish my hair weren't
       turning gray.

He guided me towards a small bin and rinsed me off.
"See how clean and soft. It's on sale," he said.

It had a light, citrusy scent.
I agreed to buy a box.

"And what are you doing about your face?"

He presented me with a box of facial cleanser.

"It will brighten your dark spots and tighten your pores."

I walked away with four boxes of skin products.

Had I not been feeling bad about being blemished and sweaty from the gym,
I might have thought to say,

*It is the rare diamond that doesn't have a flaw,
and people still buy them.*

Pluck

How did that happen,
we coo at our men,
stroking grooves on
faces
hands
shoulders
backs,
sighing as they relay
pummeling fists,
falls,
crashes.

Unless they are scars from childbirth,
it is most likely that
people stare,
ask
What happened to you
until we,
who seek desire,
surrender,
paint them over
in glossy colors,
cover them with clothing
or long hair,
like the images of unmarred skin
that surround us.

It is the bravest woman
who,
while
she learns how
to read,
to adore her scars,
burns sage,
wields swords,
beckons to her sisters:
Come. I have much to show you.

When We Answered The Call

We
wild dandelion seeds
gathered for conversation,
sacred rituals.

We grow our roots far and wide
tenderize unforgiving earth
summon nutrients from the deep
so other life can bloom.

We
are learning to take
what society
says is a shortcoming
in ourselves

put it in a box

wrap it up in pretty paper
tape the seams
decorate it with ribbons
and bows.

Sap

Thwap!

Kia had pulled and snapped my bra strap
one too many times.
The invisible dams I built in my eyes
threatened to burst.
No one was coming to rescue me
from the lunchroom,
then three more hours of sitting at a desk
in front of Kia,
so I had to save myself.
"I can't breathe,"
I gasped at one of the school aides.
She took me to the office.
I huffed, cried, and sniffled as I begged my mother
       to pick me up.
"You're getting germs all over my phone,"
the secretary snapped,
handing me a tissue and alcohol to wipe down the
       receiver.
Mother couldn't leave her desk.
She called Aunt LaVerne,
who sent Aunt Marguerite's
home health aide to pick me up,
and even as my heart and breath stopped racing,
I mimicked hyperventilation
until I was sitting on Aunt Verne's pink sofa,
wishing I was one of those girls

who had a big sister a head taller than Kia,
who was a head taller than me,
the second tallest girl in our fourth grade class.
She would put her hands on her hips
swing her right finger in Kia's face
and press it against her forehead--
You better leave my sister alone,
so Kia could sit at our white lunchroom table
with tears clogging her throat.
If only I had a big sister
to hug me and lift my chin:
*You better not let nobody hold your self-esteem
hostage*
so I wouldn't have to wait on Kia's torso
to align with her arms and legs,
for her mother to let her hair out of her braids and
frame her pretty face,
smile a hello at me when we,
at different schools,
bumped into each other on the block
and I'd wonder if she was now
one of the girls
the popular boys chased
to squeeze their butts
or if she,
like me, was swerved around
while the chased ones giggled
and I pretended not to care.

Cracked

I mostly keep my man,
our thing,
to myself
but sometimes
I wish
other people could see
the gratitude in his kisses
across the span of my shoulders,
the small of my back,
hear the roll of bass in his
You're beautiful
the
Sexy
the
Aw, sugars
when all I have done
is stride from the bed to the dresser.

I know I am more than just
this body, but
it is dangerous
that I say
yeah, right
oh, please
I'm fat
more than
thank you.

I wish I could fall in love
with the very thing
holding me all together.

"We all have a dark side. Most of us go through life avoiding direct confrontation with that aspect of ourselves, which I call the shadow self. There's a reason why. It carries a great deal of energy."

- Lorraine Toussaint

Ingress

I thought I was just going to write some poems here.
At worst
my pen might leak,
stain my fingers and hands blue or black.

"Describe your shadow self," she said.
That is like getting down on your knees
to look under somebody's
sofa
to see what they've swept underneath.

Revealing the bitterroot of me
would be like banging my shin
against the foot of my bed.

*I've gotten so good at
walking tall,
sitting straight-backed,
cross-legged,
smiling,
doling compliments,
no one would know how
I pick happy people apart in my head,
especially
gorgeous women.
If I confess,
what will these women,
my family and friends,
think of me?*

Veneer

Would she ever understand
how hard
I have worked to
glow in the dark?

My Honey Jar

My first, middle, and last name
in slow, even, curvy script
on a slip of paper.

Brown sugar at the base.
A layer of lavender for calm.
Rosemary on top of that for concentration.

Two copies of a letter:

Dear God,

*Thank you for every blessing of love and health in my
    life.*
*Please be patient with me as I learn to see beauty in
    myself and other people.*
*Please keep my arms, my hands, my legs strong and
    steady*
*while I massage my imagination with short spells of
    quiet isolation,*
swing sledgehammers at writer's block,
and stride through the light and the dark.

One copy of the letter is folded then halved and
        quartered
until I am left with a paper square.
It goes in the middle.

Cloves for my healing wounds and to fortify my liver
        and blood.
Cinnamon for balance before a layer of brown sugar
        on top.

The clink of the metal lid
against the mouth of the glass.
I light the green candle.

Press my hands together.
Read the second copy of the letter aloud.
Close my eyes against the slow, flickering burn.

Lost

Momma said I was walking at 6 months and talking at
    9 months
because I always knew
I had places to go and much to say
learned to read at 2
careened down hills on my Big Wheels
waved my arms and hooted like an owl when my
    teachers wanted answers
wrote poems and asked if I could recite them in front
    of the class
let my hair out and flung it while I danced in front of
    mirrors
told a boy that called my sister a nigger that we were
    black and damn proud of it
called myself Lady C when I thought I could rap
didn't let scraped knees and bottom-bouncing falls off
    my skateboard
keep me from learning how to pop a wheelie.
I had a wad of confidence tucked in my back pocket
    every day.

As bigger egos with
taller bodies
stronger fists
surrounded me,
shouted me down,
had throngs
that we used to call "back",
fearing black eyes
and torn-out hair,
I started slouching
and mumbling,
my eyes fixed
on the ground.

Light

We were partnered up.
Assigned to look at each other.
Write positive things on a post-it note.

I listed my partner's
kindness
determination
light in her eyes
delicate hands
beautiful curves
flame of red in her hair
pride in her Puerto Rican heritage.

My partner wrote:

Strength

(I am strong)

Dexterity

(I excel at parenting, teaching, writing)

Warmth

(I listen well and empathize)

Aliveness

(I am quietly lively)

Color coordination

(My clothes are neat and match)

Beautiful tresses

(My locs are coming in nicely)

Beautiful smile

(So my dentist says!)

Suppleness

(I have to be in the classroom!)

We smiled.
We hugged.

Weight

When we had to write down
two things
we don't like about ourselves
on another post-it note,
I wrote:

    1. Blemishes on my face
    2. Being overweight

I put the note inside
the empty shoebox
we were asked to bring
and replaced the top.

I was proud of my honesty.
Wished I could have said
I couldn't think of a single thing,

that I could transform this melancholy

over the obstinate mound of flesh around my sunken
        navel
and the imperfections on my face

into a lump of clay,
bang it with a hammer,
and sweep the dust into the bottom of this shoe box.

The Spiritual Bath

Early morning.
I scrubbed my tub clean.
Put on a small pot of water to boil.
Placed leaves of
sage
basil
hyssop
white willow to cleanse the brain,
cinnamon and peppermint to stimulate the circulation,
to steep for 30 minutes
while I sat on my sofa waiting for
the orange glow of sunrise to stream through my
        window.
When it was time, I strained the leaves and put them
        in a bowl.
Put aside the herb-infused water for tea.
Covered it to keep warm.

Filled the tub halfway with warm water.
Placed the herbs in it with three drops of myrrh oil for
fragrance and cleansing.
Disrobed.
Sat.

Closed my eyes.
Deeply inhaled the sharp notes of the herbs.
Seven times I cupped the water in my hands,
let it drip down my
head
face
throat
heart
navel
and said my affirmation:

Good morning. I am thankful to be a sacred beautiful daughter of God.

Patted myself dry.
Smoothed my skin with lavender-scented lotion.
Put on a white dress and a white headwrap.
Dropped the juice of half a fresh lemon, 3 teaspoons of honey in my tea.

On My Knees

If I must come back
Please return me in this same butter-soft body
adorned by this same clove-brown hair that glows
      amber in the light
but with blue flame in my ribs.

Please return me in this same butter-soft body.
A thirst only for water
but with blue flame in my ribs.
A hunger only for food.

A thirst only for water,
clangorous voice ringing nipple to nipple.
A hunger only for food.
Let those like me,

clangorous voices ringing nipple to nipple,
with flawed skin and self-esteem,
let those like me,
hear how to forge an interior love in spite of it all,

with flawed skin and self-esteem,
adorned by this same clove-brown hair that glows
      amber in the light,
hear how to forge an interior love in spite of it all.
If I must come back.

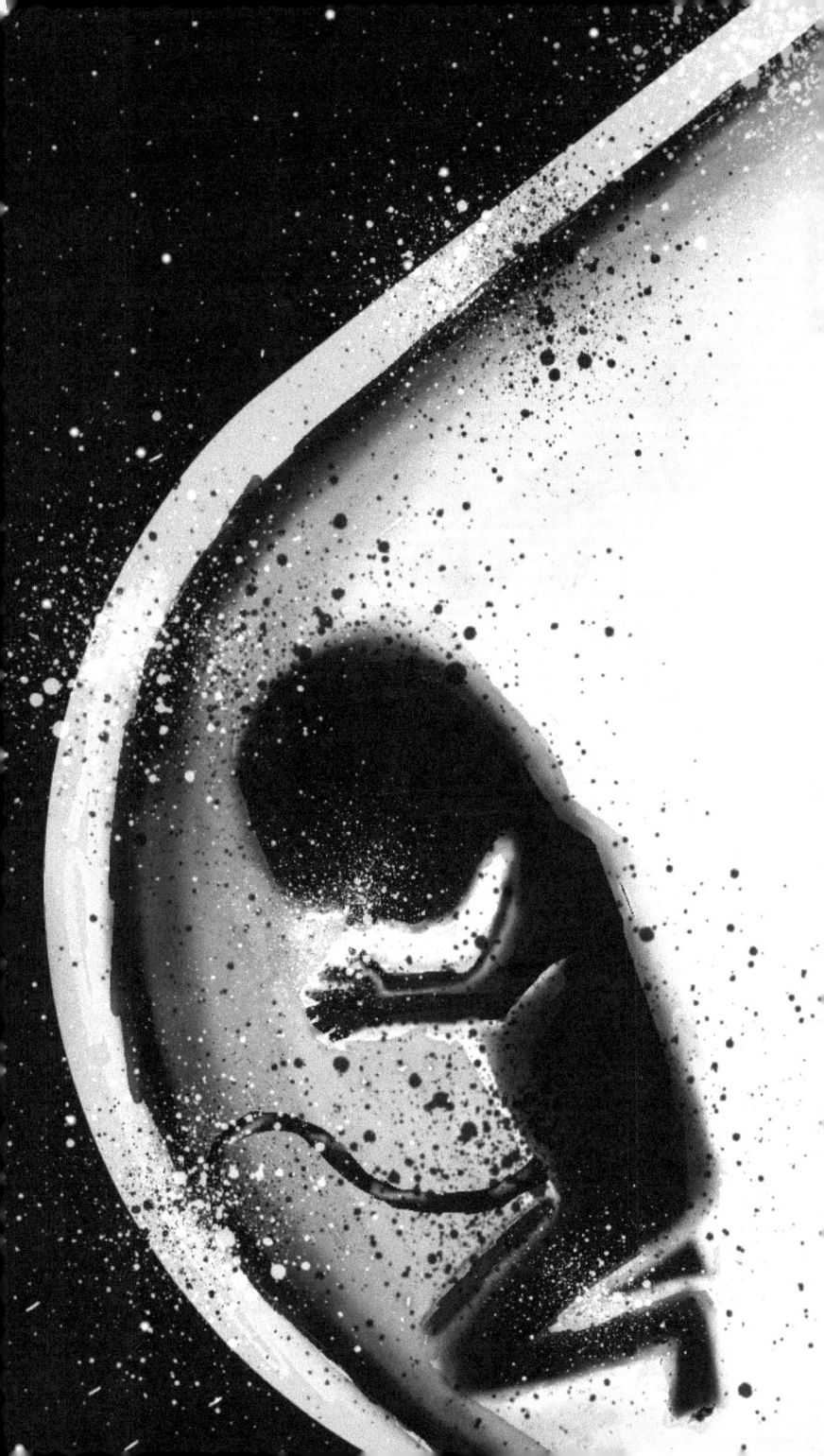

If God were to pray over you,
what would She say?

Grace

My daughters,
dress your sister like Olokun.

Make her a crown of white seashells.
Craft a bouquet of blue coral.

Adorn her face, but only with water-based makeup.
Burnish her face with mahogany foundation.

Silver and blue eyeshadow below her eyebrows.
Line her lips and eyes in sky and royal blue.

Cajole her eyelashes with mascara out/up into
      voluptuous curves.
Dust her cheeks with rosy blush.

Stipple her cheekbones and chin with silver dots.
Hang a sparkling earring in each earlobe.

Bedaub her chest and shoulders with soft shea oil
and sprinkle her with silver glitter.

Bedrape her with white, sheer blue fabric.
Have her sit beneath the blue coral bouquet.

Instruct her to thrust her shoulders back, bosom
      forward.
Arrange the white lights around her until she is in
      proper focus.

Give her a silver tray arrayed with silver jewelry
and beaded blue necklaces to hold.

I feel beautiful.

Sermon

You still don't know how to pair "I am" with *beautiful*
    instead of "I feel".
And what happens after you wash away the makeup?

What you must do first is realize:

        You are
            bursts of
            green
            blue
            white
            yellow
            shimmy-shaking,
            then
            slow waltzing
            into
            orange.
            Red.

        You are the
            blaze
            bloat
            and fall
            of
            hydrogen,
            helium,
            cast into
            carbon
            nitrogen
            oxygen
            iron
            sulfur.

I AM *BEAUTIFUL*.

feel

Wonder

*We used to be stars?
Is that why
we look to the heavens,
crave love
and attention
the way we do?*

**What obstructs
the doorway
between Spirit
and your skin?**

War On Canvas

My high school graduation picture is retouched proof
    of what I could have been.
In it, instead of she-would-be-pretty-if,
my almond eyes are portals of beauty,
my smile glimmers like sunlight on a lake at high
    noon,
my skin is the
clear
smooth medium brown
it was until I was nine.
At 10,
T-zone.
Mini eruptions on forehead/temples/cheeks.
Sole sufferer in my circle of friends.
One day, I ran up to my father who was greeting a
    family friend.
Oh Melvin, her skin.
Mommy said her mother's father's people had bad
    skin.
A friend's mother squeezed my pimples for half an
hour,
leaving me with mini-geysers leaking blood. Pus.
Scars.
My first boyfriend at 14,
the one who couldn't believe a virgin like me could
    kiss so well,
backed away from me when his friend said:
The only thing that's wrong with that girl is her face.
There are no pretty girls in your class, my
    clear-skinned cousin once said.
My next boyfriend: *Those girls at the Rucker are bad.*
    Sorry, you couldn't compete with 'em.
Fed up with my longing in mirrors, Daddy threw away
my Fruit Loops.
Lost it when I complained.

If you didn't eat that stuff, you'd be better looking.
A doctor promised my skin would clear up pretty if I ate fresh-cut pineapple.

pHisoderm.

Clearasil.

Cernitin America's wash and toner that Daddy used to sell, and gave to me.

Noxzema.

Apricot scrub.

Lemon and egg, clay facial masks squeezed but never quite shrunk my pores.

Ambi ads with flawless brown women in *Essence* magazine. Bought a tube.

Used it a few times but feared uneven discoloration.
My face healed in my twenties, but still bore the scars.
Foundation felt like smeared butter across my face so I kept it nude.
Just arched my brows with a brush and a little color on my lips.

A bunch of us were playing a game once.
The card read, "What would you change if you could?"

I think I said wearing glasses.
My friend said, *I thought you'd say your skin.*
In front of her friends, her man.
No one came to my defense. Not even me.

Damn this
Bad
Bad
Bad
Bad
Bad
Bad
Bad
Bad skin.

Some have tattooed teardrops on their faces to call out
    their pain.
In my thirties some of my poppin' melanocytes
    loitered right above my cheekbones.
Black moles--like my mother and grandmother had--
    grew too close to my eyes to be removed.
Arrayed themselves like teardrops.
The biggest two underneath my left eye.
Miniature lava rocks.
Maybe each mole is someone I've lost.
I won't count them. I can't think about who/what else I
    may lose.
Death comes for us all but don't tell me when or how.

Was thankful for cell phone cameras.
If I had to be photographed,
I knew best
how to capture myself under
soft, white, 40-watt light--
my almond eyes and smile glimmering
like sunlight on a lake at high noon,
and my skin is
clear,
smooth medium brown.
But there is something about 40 and fuck it.
Another man, who wanted a gem on his arm, lost me.
In my moving on, I rediscovered poetry.
Learned how to dance.
In those caliginous lounges and nightclubs,
people took pictures with me in them.
My smile glimmering.

A stunner made of stardust.
Like my mother and grandmother and her father's
people.

I bathe my face with black soap and water.
They do quiet work across my forehead, temples, and cheeks.
There are still scars but
now that I know of Olokun and the ocean,
how they protect the sons and daughters of the Motherland that were tossed overboard,
and the brave ones who couldn't swim all the way back to her shores,
I think of my skin like the ocean floor,
with its seamounts and guyots.
I too, am
deep,
often silent,
not easily knowable.

I have stopped trying to smother and strangle my moles,
my rocks of lava.

People buy lava rock jewelry
to possess the fire, the strength, the courage
that naturally sits beneath my eyes.

No more running from dim light.
I, and the best kind of people, don't need soft, 40-watt white light to see my beauty.

My man asked me for the privilege of photographing me.

I stood before him
wearing nothing
but cowrie shell earrings
and ruby red lipstick.

He dipped a brush into a bottle of golden glitter,
anointed me
forehead to cheek,
cheek to shoulder,
areola to areola,
to navel,
to knees,
to toes.

In front of his black satin backdrop,
he had me
gazing
grinning
spinning in half circles,
sucking in nothing.
Oh yeah.
Just like that.

After he uploaded the pictures onto my computer,
I closed my door
turned off the lights to look
at the unretouched proofs.

Saw a stunner made of stardust.
The surface of my face like the ocean floor.
Beauty in dim light.

My skin.
This boss
boss
Bad
Bad
Bad
Bad
Bad
Bad-ass skin.

Manna

Thumping of palms and fingertips
against the center and edges of a djembe,
and my shimmying hips.

the crunch of communion wafers and the tang of grape
juice
after private confessions.
Salt water on my tongue.

Breathing into my nose from my diaphragm,
out through my mouth.
Downward facing dog
Cobra
Mountain pose
Half spinal twists
Lotus,
hands at rest on thighs.
Closed eyes.
Gongs and chimes caressing ear drums,
ballast stilling bluster
and thunder behind my eyes.

Pass It On

We
black
and brown
girls
should have been
commanded
to memorize
and recite
Psalm 139
in Sunday school

and

before every sundown
stomp our feet
clap our hands:

All praises due to God,
I'm fearfully, wonderfully made!

Next

Something else Ms. Hansberry and I share besides
    logophilia:
I love to stand by the banks
of rivers, lakes, ocean shores.
I jump into pools.
Never been tender-headed,
afraid of shrinkage,
or burdened by the
washing, oiling, combing, drying,
twisting, braiding, palm rolling after.

My sister,
friends from across the courtyard,
and I,
figured out how to float, but
all I can do is lie

belly flat on top of the water
hold my arms straight as rods
kick myself forward
eyes closed
for as long as I can hold my breath,

or on my back
and flutter my legs for a minute or two
before I begin to sink.

Been too afraid to
open my eyes under water to risk the sting of chlorine
       or salt
open my mouth to inhale/exhale
for the breaststroke, but
there is nothing else as pure
or as soft
on my skin
as water.

                                   It is time
                            I learn how to swim.

Afterword

© Photograph by Peggy Robles-Alvarado
Photo edited by Tamara G. Saliva

During one of her "More Than Just" project workshops, Peggy Robles-Alvarado implored me to explore Olokun. She is an orisha from the Yoruba faith associated with rebirth, renewal, healing, wealth and abundance. She is considered to be androgynous and her name means owner of the ocean. She is associated with the deepest part of the ocean where there is very little light.

As I reflected upon my decades-long mourning of my skin's imperfections and struggle to believe I am outwardly beautiful, I was challenged to think about the depths and the darkness of the ocean's bottom. Just as the darkness of the ocean makes it difficult for us to see how it teems with marine life, my insecurity obscured my ability to see my self-worth.

In preparation for my photo shoot for "More Than Just", I was adorned with make-up and garb in shades of blue, one of Olokun's colors. The crown of seashells that was placed on my head represent the seashells that decorate the terracotta pot that is believed to be Olokun's home and keeper of her secrets. The jewels I wore symbolize hidden treasures of the ocean.

I emerged from the project grateful for my renewed confidence and faith in myself. Now that I am approaching the half-century mark, I think about the beauty and strength of my grandmothers, mother and aunts and strive to age and exist as gracefully and naturally as they.

I am hopeful that this book will inspire people who have similarly struggled with self-esteem to dive in, explore the roots of their self-doubt, and arise to the surface, born anew.

Carla M. Cherry is an English teacher from New York. Her poems have appeared in anthologies, journals, and litzines such as *Anderbo, Eunoia Review, Dissident Voice, Random Sample Review, MemoryHouse, Bop Dead City, Terra Preta Review, Synaeresis, Ariel Chart, Variety Pack, and Anti-Heroin Chic.* She has published four other books of poetry through Wasteland Press: *Gnat Feathers and Butterfly Wings* (2008), *Thirty Dollars and a Bowl of Soup* (2017), *Honeysuckle Me* (2017), and *These Pearls Are Real* (2018). A graduate of Spelman College, New York University, and Lehman College, she is pursuing her Master of Fine Arts in Creative Writing at the City College of New York.

www.ingramcontent.com/pod-product-compliance
Lightning Source LLC
Chambersburg PA
CBHW062023290426
44108CB00024B/2761